MARKETING FOR PROFESSIONAL ARTISTS

In The Second Decade Of The 21st Century

Peter K Worsley

ISBN: 1493527363
ISBN-13: 978-1493527366

Library of Congress Control Number: 2014900067
CreateSpace Independent Publishing Platform
North Charleston, South Carolina

DEDICATION

This book is dedicated to my wife, Mary, for all of the patience
and support she provides me in my many endeavors.

CONTENTS

ACKNOWLEDGMENTS

I am indebted to my good friend Juliana Minsky for her in-depth critique of my early draft. I'd also like to acknowledge the feedback I received from my workshop participants, plus helpful comments from Gary Silverstein and my editors, Amelia and Allan. All have helped to bring this book to completion.

PREFACE

I first started painting seriously after I retired in 1996. This followed nearly fifty years of working in industry, mostly in marketing and communication.

Even after seventeen years of trying to become a successful professional fine artist painter, it is hard to keep what I learned in the world of industry from intruding into my painting world. After talking to other artists I realized that many prospective professional artists do not know what it takes to market their artworks. Also, in this rapidly changing environment of the Internet and other related means of communication, the so-called "tried and true methods" of yesteryear are no longer adequate.

Upon reaching the age of eighty-four, and with the impending threat of chronic health issues hovering over me, I decided that my insight into this area of artistry and marketing gave me an opportunity to give back to the art community.

I prepared a detailed outline and tried it out at a series of intimate small-group discussion workshops in my living room. This outline, feedback from these workshops, and my research with many online resources are the roots from which this book grew.

For those of a technical mindset, the draft was prepared using Apple Pages on an iPad 1, transferred via iCloud to an iMac, and pasted into a Microsoft Word document template.

The book describes what I have learned about the marketing decisions and tools facing the professional artist in the second decade of the twenty-first century.

—*Peter Worsley, fine artist painter, marketer, and published author,*
January 2014

INTRODUCTION

If you consider yourself to be in the "art" business, or even the "art publishing" business, you are starting off on the wrong foot and headed up the wrong path. Today, to be a professional visual artist, you must be in the business of building, nurturing, and replenishing a direct-buying collector base. In addition, you may be part of a network of galleries, individuals, and businesses that sell art.

Very few artists have the self-confidence and strength of mind that it takes to be a successful professional. This book discusses what it takes. When you have read the book, you may decide that to be a professional artist requires too much commitment. [1] However, if you feel adventurous, I provide hints as to where to start.

As with most freelance businesses, you should be prepared to devote about a third of your time to marketing. The value of this commitment has stood the test of time. Do less, and you will find yourself building an inventory of artwork that nobody wants.

Marketing is the process of communication between you and other people. Perhaps it is better to restate that as:

Art marketing is communicating information about yourself and your artwork to others.

In today's art world, you are intimately attached to your artwork. A collector of art is just as interested in the creator of the artwork as the artwork itself. You, the artist, are forever connected to your artworks.

Like many things today, contemporary communication processes are evolving and frequently changing. As a result, the methods of marketing your artwork are an ever-changing process. This is discussed in great detail in the chapters that follow.

The traditional marketing processes that dominated the twentieth century are often described as the "Madison Avenue" approach. They are caricatured by popular TV programs such as *Mad Men*, in print, or on film in such classics as *The Man in the Gray Flannel Suit*.

During that period, marketing consisted of the creation of avenues of communication for the seller. These avenues were used to blast campaigns, each trying to convince the public to buy the client's product or service. Often this entailed the expenditure of lots of money, with big commissions flowing to the advertising agencies that initiated and managed the processes.

This process has been described as the "hit the buyer on the head" approach to gain the prospect's attention.

Today you have to entice a prospective collector to notice you and persuade him to volunteer to become entangled in your web of seduction. After the collector is in love with your artwork, you have to close the sale to get paid.

This book is divided into two parts. The early chapters introduce you to art marketing as it is today, and the later chapters discuss contemporary marketing tools you will be using.

If you wish to explore this topic in more detail, I've included endnotes to related sources throughout the book.

1. BRANDING

The problem of being noticed:

A recent survey indicated that some four million people in the United States call themselves artists. Of these, the 2000 census identified some 250,000 who call themselves professional artists—that is, artists who are trying to make a living from selling their artwork. (This statistic does not include photographers, designers, or architects.) [2]

Your principal challenge is to distinguish yourself from the sea of other artists around you.

What is unique about me?

This difficult question is a useful exercise. It is also your best starting point: "What is unique about me and/or my work?" Ask others who know you and your artwork this question.

Your uniqueness may come from your color palette, your subject matter, your brush strokes, your materials, or many other things.

Think of people whom you regard as successful professional artists, living or dead. Usually their artwork has something that instantly allows you to recognize the artist. Here are some examples: Amedeo Modigliani with his elongated figures, Van Gogh with his brush strokes and colors, Henry Moore with his bulky flowing sculptures, or contemporary artists, such as Jeff Koons, with his shiny balloon shaped figures.

Again, ask yourself, when you see their artwork, why do you automatically know that is the work of that artist?

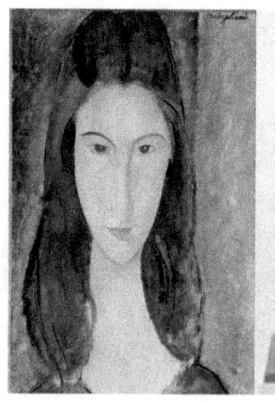 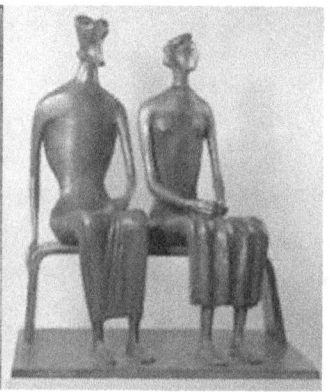

Amedeo Modigliani   Henry Moore

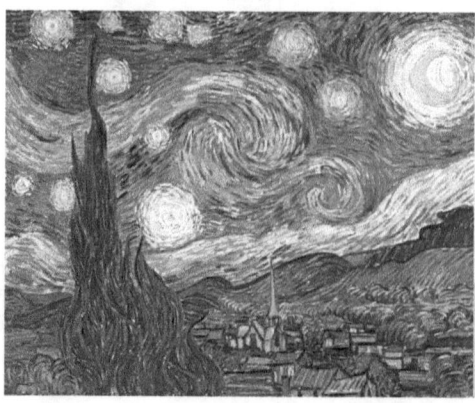 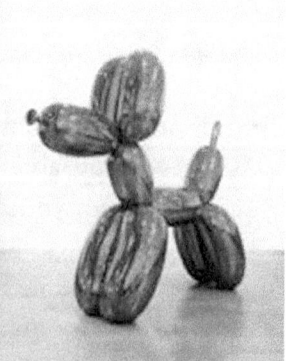

Van Gogh   Jeff Koons

This distinction is what is known in the marketing world as a "brand."

As an individual artist, it is likely that you do not have an established brand. But to gain customers—I like to call them "collectors"—you must create a brand to distinguish yourself from the crowd.

Your brand, however, should not be focused on you. It should be focused on attracting collectors. The statement, "My brand is 'Artwork That Begs to Be Touched,' immediately says something unique and connects with potential buyers.

Some brand phrases are too generic and too vague to set you apart. You might call yourself the "best western artist in America," but so what? Who compared you to other western artists? Does this statement connect with potential buyers?

On the other hand, if you describe your western art by saying, "My brand is burned onto every painting," that's something tangible for people to remember. You're the artist who uses a branding iron to sign your work. Now that would certainly set you apart from the herd!

Artist Thomas Kinkade used the brand "Painter of Light" as his defining statement. His brand explained him and his art in a short, powerful sentence. Because he was so well branded, everyone knew who he was. [3]

Your brand:

Your brand is what you are going to be known for. Good branding is the act of becoming known for something that you do. Good branding positions you above any competitor. A brand + your name + your artwork results in something that makes you unique.

Without such a brand, it will be hard for you to sell your artworks. Your brand becomes a familiar "statement" by which your collectors increase their acceptance of your artwork.

Branding not only distinguishes you from the masses but also builds trust or credibility in the eyes of your collectors.

Branding is a matter of:
1. Know me,
2. Like me,
3. Trust me,
4. and the most important of all,
5. Pay me.

Part of your branding is a need to have a cohesive look. This must exist across all your artwork.

Using your brand:

Once established, your brand must be spread across all your supporting tools: the look and signature of your emails, your website; your domain name; your user names, your logo, your color schemes, your stationery, your thank-you notes. Make sure your brand appears everywhere.

A later chapter of this book discusses your "elevator pitch." This is directly tied to your brand. My elevator pitch is, "I paint ordinary people, doing everyday things, at interesting places."

In summary:

1. Branding builds a differentiation between you and others.
2. It builds a base of relevance for your collectors' expectations.

3. It helps establish esteem for the quality of your work.
4. It creates an awareness of how you are perceived by your collector—in other words, "trust."

Here is where to start: "What is unique about your artwork?"

2. OUTBOUND MARKETING

Outbound marketing is based upon the traditional marketing processes that dominated the twentieth century. However, these processes are modified to support the "inbound marketing" processes discussed in the next chapter. Today we talk about marketing with your brain rather than your wallet.

As in earlier times, today's outbound marketing consists of building communication channels. But instead of blasting the buying prospects, you gain their permission to send carefully crafted messages loaded with interesting and instructive content.

Your message:

Almost nobody reads *People* magazine for the advertisements. Nobody goes home eagerly anticipating junk mail. Many people have disconnected their hardwired phone to avoid the sales pitch phone calls that arrive just as they are sitting down to dinner. [4]

Today, potential collectors—the recipients of your messages—are inundated every day with messages from thousands, if not millions, of "spammers" who are trying to bend their ears. Your prospective collectors, like most of us, have learned to turn off this background noise—and with it, unfortunately, your message.

To be heard, your message has to be attractive to the recipient. It has to be part of "permissive communications"—something the recipient wants to hear (or read).

Permission marketing is like dating. It turns strangers into friends, and friends into lifetime collectors. [4]

Today your target audience consists of people who have said to you, "I like what you are doing, saying, or making. Please keep me informed." They may be people who have talked with you at your art events, been referred to you by trusted friends, read your emails or blog, viewed your activity on social media, or somehow landed on your website. They have specifically requested to receive your messages. So when your crafted message arrives, they are primed to open and read it.

Recently, Chuck Green, who issues a biweekly newsletter about graphic design [5], wrote:

> I got an email from a reputable company recently that said, "Hi Chuck, I'd like to send business your way. If you're interested, simply add yourself to my network below." (With a link.)
>
> Typically, I'd assume it was a canned offer, but this was from a reputable, well respected organization, and they addressed me with, "Hi Chuck."
>
> So I answered back with: "Thanks, what type of project?" And a representative of the business replied, "This was a little PR attempt in trying to get us noticed. I apologize if it wasn't clear."

As far as I'm concerned, it was clear. This message made an explicit offer, "to send business (my way)," and that was not true. Not a big deal, just a reminder that social networking comes with consequences. If we use meaningful words to make meaningless offers, we diminish communication."

We will discuss crafting your message in much more detail in later Chapters.

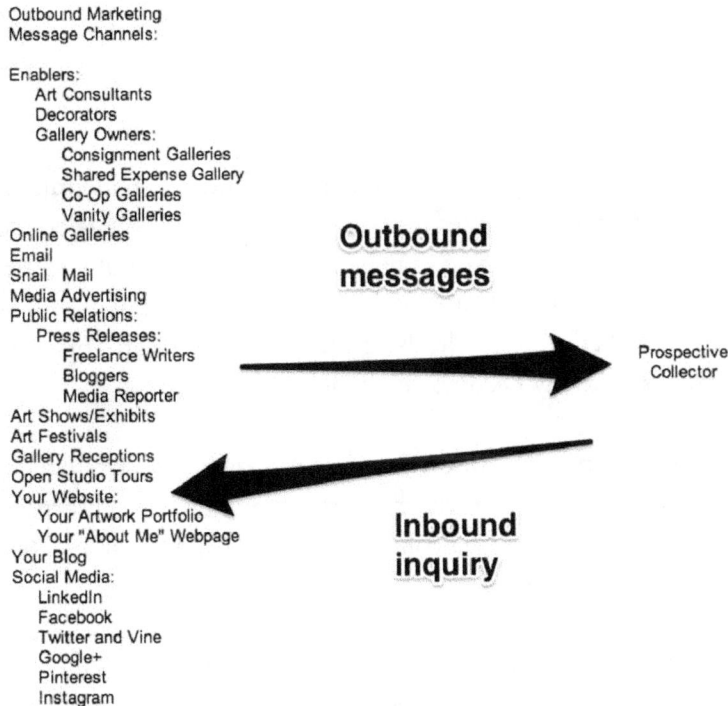

Many outbound message channels:

Outbound marketing requires you to present a "face" to the outside world that represents you and your brand, accompanied by lots of interesting content and messages.

9

Inbound marketing (discussed in the next chapter) is dealing with the response to your outbound messages, hopefully steering them toward a successful interaction and maybe a sale.

You can use a variety of outbound message channels to send your message. Some channels—enablers, galleries, email, and snail mail—are clearly directed, while others such as social media are more passive. With regard to social media, when your message is found by a prospective collector, this encourages contact with you, often through your website.

Leads, collectors, and enablers:

An outbound marketing goal is to build a list of "leads" that contain the names and (email) addresses of permissive prospective collectors. These collectors are people who may be open to your carefully crafted conversations or messages. With the help of email and snail mail message channels, you will educate the leads about you and your artwork, so that the leads may eventually become collectors.

Your list of leads should include existing as well as prospective collectors of your artworks. Any person who has already purchased your artwork for personal enjoyment is already a collector and, at the same time, a prime candidate to purchase more.

"Enablers" are people who may assist you in reaching potential collectors. They may be art consultants, decorators, dealers, or gallery owners.

Art consultants and decorators, for a fee, help their clients find artwork for their projects (homes, offices, and industrial and medical facilities). Art consultants offer advice to their clients for large and small purchases but are very selective in the artwork they desire. The artwork has to fit the theme of the project.

Generally, art consultants and decorators look at your artworks as decorative items. Only occasionally may they be interested in an artwork as an investment for their client. It is unlikely that their client will fall in love with your artwork and become a repeat collector.

Generally a dealer buys only for himself. He may have a private gallery where he shows his purchased artworks to his group of prospective collectors. Dealers frequently work in the secondary market. That is, they buy your artwork from the original collector (or often from a collector's estate) and put your artwork up for resale.

Usually you have to be a well-known artist with a "name" to be of interest to a dealer.

B&M (bricks and mortar) consignment galleries as message channels:

Galleries, both B&M and online, may be bridges to existing and potential collectors. B&M gallery owners sometimes buy artworks, but more generally they take your artwork on consignment.

Until recently, almost all B&M galleries operated on a contingent fee basis. They took in your artwork and tried to sell it, sharing their sales income with you through a commission arrangement. [6]

Since any B&M gallery owner has a high overhead, he or she is looking to move your artwork as soon as possible. Usually the gallery owner has a pretty good idea of who will eventually buy your artwork, before they get interested in talking with you.

Usually the gallery owner has his own list of potential collectors. Both dealers and gallery owners protect their lists and usually do not want to share their collector contact data with you.

B&M shared expenses galleries as message channels:

With the slowdown in sales through consignment galleries over the last few years, some B&M (and online) galleries will ask you to share the risk. They will request some money up front to help cover their expenses. In return, they offer to work on a lower commission scale. Any gallery that operates on a shared-expenses basis has less incentive to move your artwork.

One popular low-end version of this style of gallery is the "co-op gallery." Usually these galleries are started by a group of artists getting together on a volunteer basis and sharing expenses. There are many variations. Co-op galleries have been around for years, and they exist in numerous communities across the country. "Hanging fees" and commissions are usually low, and you may be asked to participate in the operation of the gallery. Many professional artists, including myself, started in such a gallery, and some continue to show their work there. [7]

At the other end of the scale, beware of the "vanity gallery." This gallery owner will welcome you with open arms and give you a great song and dance about the values of his gallery, his wonderful regular "openings" and "events," and how you will receive great exposure. Often the gallery owner has pictures and videos of these affairs.

For all this, the gallery owner will offer you a few feet of wall space at a "modest" few hundred (or thousand) dollars a month, quarter, or year. The vanity gallery makes all of its money from your prepayment fees, and virtually none from sales commissions. In addition, you have to pay to ship your artwork to the gallery (and back again, when it is still unsold and you decide you have had enough).

Typically the large crowd you see at their events are other artists who have been invited to attend, not prospective collectors. [8]

B&M gallery changes and their effect on your message channels:

As with many other things, in good times and bad, 10 percent of the galleries do 90 percent of the business, with perhaps 1 percent of the artists selling 90 percent of the art. [9]

The rise in popularity of the Internet, as well as poor economic times, have produced a decline in business for the B&M galleries. Collectors of an artist who have purchased their artwork before, and who have built up some trust in the artist's artwork, are tempted to bypass the gallery where they purchased the original artwork and negotiate directly with the artist.

The ease of using the Internet to locate and buy directly from the artist, and the rise of online galleries that have a low overhead, are forcing many B&M galleries out of business.

However, this is not happening to all galleries. There are always some collectors who want the gallery owner to do the selective screening and the artist interface tasks, and at the same time give the collector an opportunity to "touch" the product before purchasing it.

Online galleries as message channels:

Setting up and operating an online gallery may be inexpensive, and as a result the Internet is swamped with such galleries. Most B&M galleries have set up their own online galleries, and many are doing good business through those channels. The British gallery Saatchi reports that they sell more art online in a month than most B&M galleries do in a year. [10]

But actually setting up an effective online gallery can be expensive. To be successful, the gallery must have its own outbound marketing program. As is discussed later, what matters at any website, including your own and the online gallery's, is the number of unique visitors.

An online gallery without traffic from visitors is not going to do you much good. Of course, what really matters is the number of sales. But few online galleries publicize either of these statistics. Beware of galleries that are not open about their traffic numbers.

Some online galleries charge you to exhibit your artwork, just like shared-expenses B&M galleries. Commission rates vary over a wide range.

Many online galleries target specific market price ranges. Some go for the print market, often offering prints of paintings and illustrations that are copyright-free at low prices. Other online galleries are interested only in the higher-priced "name" artist market. There are online galleries for every kind of market.

With the recent launch of Amazon Art in partnership with 150 US dealers, the marketplace may be expected to change further. [11]

Email message channel:

This is by far the most popular method of business message communication. [12] Keep an eye, though, on texting and messaging, as they are very popular with young people, and you should expect these communication methods to spread into the business world as these youngsters move along their career paths.

This important communication channel, and how to use it, are discussed in more detail in a later chapter.

Snail mail and printed material as a message channel:

Conventional mail, or "snail mail," still has its place in outgoing marketing. It tends to be an expensive path. But a nicely designed color postcard invitation to an art event, or a personalized thank-you note, can have considerable impact.

Also, business cards, brochures, leaflets, and bookmarks all have their value. Be sure to include your website address on the mailing piece, so that people can reach you. Modern Postcard's website (http://www. modernpostcard.com) has many helpful aids you can use when you are exploring these paths.

QR (Quick Response) codes are a recent tool consisting of black modules (square dots) arranged in a square grid on a white background. A prospective collector with a smartphone and a suitable application may scan the code printed on your material and be taken directly to your website landing page or your email signup page. [12] I display a QR code for my website address on nearly all of my printed materials.

To read QR codes, I use the "QwikScan" application on my iPhone. To create QR codes, the emailing application, MailChimp (http://www. mailchimp.com) (discussed in a later chapter) has a feature under its "lists" section to create a QR code that, when read, automatically sends people to its list signup page. I can use the tool QRStuff (http://www. qrstuff.com) to create almost any QR code.

When using QR codes, do not expect too much: recent studies indicate that few people actually click through using a QR code. [13]

Media advertising message channel:

The purchasing of advertisements in a suitable media may still have its place. Communication via advertisements tends to be an expensive way to reach your audience. The most difficult part when using this channel is in determining how many of the media readers/viewers are prospective collectors. It is even more difficult to determine how many will actually view your advertisement.

The declining circulation of traditional newspapers and magazines means that you have to look carefully at who is actually reading the media in which you might advertise.

Reader/viewer demographics are always hard to obtain from media organizations, and few of those organizations can tell you if they are prospective collectors. Think carefully about those magazines that contain multiple pages of advertisements, interleaved with occasional stories. Look at your own habits when reading these media. How often do you look at the ads?

Similar problems exist with online advertising. Who looks at the ads that pop up on a website, or appear along the top or bottom of your smartphone? (For a different perspective, see the discussion about Google Ads in a later chapter.)

Public relations message channel:

This includes many things. The press releases of the past attempted to reach various and fairly well-defined assignment editors, producers, and reporters. Any of them might be persuaded to present your story through their media to the end readers/viewers. I have memories, from years ago, of dropping off a bottle of Scotch or a gift package at the offices of our favorite reporters, just before the holidays.

Today, however, press releases are no longer about winning over the hearts and minds of some six key reporters. Public relations is about telling a compelling story to the world that catches the mind of a blogger, freelance art writer, or maybe an overloaded mainstream media reporter. Hopefully their rewritten story will encourage a flow of inbound marketing and get their readers to visit your art event or, at the very least, your website.

Art exhibits, shows, festivals, etc., as message channels:

Exhibits at art shows, art festivals, gallery receptions, and open studio tours give you an opportunity to interact directly with prospective collectors. A later chapter includes a discussion on how to collect leads to build your email lists from such contacts.

Before participating in this type of event, satisfy yourself that the art exhibit connects to the type of prospective collector for your artwork. Are the other artworks on show in your price range? Is the show for crafts or professional fine art? Will the traffic going through the exhibit include your prospective collectors, or will most of the traffic consist of collectors of a different type of art?

When participating, remember that you are always on show. Always ensure that you are presenting a professional image when your prospective collectors are around. They may be looking at you from a distance, but your image is always part of your message. You are continually building, or losing, trust with your prospective collectors.

Your website as a message channel:

An artist's website has a special place in today's outbound marketing. It provides static messages about you and your artwork and, at the same time, is the target of most inbound marketing communications (as discussed in the next and later chapters).

For most artists, the website is the essential centerpiece of the entire marketing effort. It is the window through which the prospective collector will view your artwork skills—and you.

For many artists, the website is a showcase for available artwork. The site also tells a prospective collector how he or she may reach you, and how to follow your progress.

Today, no professional artist can expect to succeed without a website. The structure, design, and choices for your website are discussed in detail in a later chapter.

Your blog as a message channel:

A blog is a great and professional way to pass along information about you and your artwork. It is an online journal that must be frequently updated, though the updates may be short.

Content is key, and a blog is very time-consuming to create and maintain. [14] [15]

The two popular free blogging services WordPress and Blogger [16] will help you on your way. I have attempted blogging several times, but have never found the time needed to be justified in using a blog for promoting my artworks over other marketing channels.

However, I have started a blog about this book (http://peterworsleymarketingbook.wordpress.com) where you may comment about the book's content, obtain links to new material, updates to the links in the notes, read my afterthoughts, and perhaps give me a formal review.

Social media as messaging channels:

Social media are a wide group of digital networking tools that may be used to drive traffic to your website. There you may engage your visitors and capture the email addresses of permissive prospective collectors.

Ever since businesses and organizations started using Facebook and Twitter, there's been an ongoing debate about the roles of email and social media. As social media channels continue to change their algorithms, some professionals are noticing that, more than ever, only email gives them the powerful and consistent link with their audiences that they need.

Even so, you won't hear talk anytime soon about the death of social media. All of the ways that you communicate and interact with your audience are important. Facebook and Twitter (discussed below) help you build relationships and get to know your fans, followers, and prospective collectors even better. This, in turn, makes it easier to talk to them like human beings in your email campaigns.

Most of the social media tools are relatively new. Some are more proven than others. Many more will come, and many may fade. Each tool is trying to establish a method of making money to sustain itself As a result, these social media tools continually "remake" themselves.

All of the tools are constantly modifying their services to meet challenges from their competition and to boost their attractiveness to advertisers.

These changes may not always be in your favor. You need to watch all of them carefully.

To use most social media effectively, you have to display data about yourself and your artworks, and then gather followers or connections that may lead to prospective collectors directly contacting your website, your artwork, or even yourself.

To keep these followers or connections interested, you must continuously feed quality content through your social media tools. For some channels, this may be required as frequently as every day.

As will be discussed in a later chapter, producing quality content is hard work. Without the care and feeding of attractive, entertaining, and useful content, most followers and connections will wither away. Like blogging, this is very time-consuming.

Do not spam others with messages about yourself or your artwork. Nothing will void all your good work on content as quickly as spamming, even if it's accidental. Avoid using personal comments and images. Restrict your messages, comments, and images to things that may be of interest to your potential collectors. Always think and act as the professional that you are.

Below are some of today's common social media tools. Watch carefully, for other tools will arise and should be considered as time goes on.

LinkedIn as a message channel:

LinkedIn (http:// www.linkedIn.com) is a free online service—they have a paid premium service, but you probably don't need it—where potential collectors may look for detailed information about you. It is the professional artist's personal advertisement, and it's very important in your marketing toolkit.

LinkedIn comes in two forms: a personal page and a company page. As a professional artist, you need both, for you are both: an individual as the artist, and a company (think brand) as the producer of your artwork.

You should fill out your résumé and biography in detail, even if some of it is not about you as an artist. Go all the way back to your schooling.

If you join LinkedIn, take a look at my LinkedIn page (http://tinyurl. com/pwqyvan). (There were seventeen Peter Worsleys the last time I looked, but I am the only artist.) I list myself under all of my artist's hats. You never know how someone may be searching. Always present your best professional image. This is the chance to show all that you can do.

LinkedIn has many discussion groups. I have joined several, particularly those involving collectors. From time to time I join in and contribute my thoughts. It is a great way to become known.

One of the best ways to be found on LinkedIn is to build up your own network of connections in a strategic manner. LinkedIn values both the depth and breadth of your network when it prioritizes your name in search results and recommended connections. This means that every new connection is an opportunity to enhance your visibility with your target audience of prospective collectors.

Connect with people with whom you have a real reason to connect—for example, anyone whom you know and respect in the art business world. Start with fellow artists; collectors you know; people who work in the art industry; vendors; complimentary service providers; and, of course, prospective collectors.

But be aware of "connection shoppers." Sometimes I receive an invite from someone with five hundred-plus connections. I know that he cares little about me professionally, only as another trophy for the connections collection.

When you invite a person to connect, LinkedIn will prompt you to clarify how you know the individual. While it's tempting to send an invite with the default message ("I'd like to add you to my professional network on LinkedIn"), stop and take the time to include a personalized note and a reason for why you'd like to connect. Explain who you are and why you're interested in connecting.

For each new connection, your network exposure grows exponentially. Every person in your network has the opportunity to interact with your personal profile and professional (company) page, and to amplify your presence through his or her own network.

Nothing impacts people's perceptions and behavior like the recommendation of a trusted friend or colleague. When you post content to your personal profile or your company page, your connections can "like," share, or comment on your updates, which "amplifies" your message to their entire first-degree networks. And as your connections amplify your posts across LinkedIn, you have the chance to build relationships with even more members who discover you through the recommendation of a close contact.

To make this work, optimize your personal profile and professional (company) page, and actively update, discuss, and share valuable content that your network will find interesting and informative. Also consider sharing articles and ideas with connections whom you know will take a specific interest. The more personalized and targeted your network interactions are, the stronger your presence will be within your network!

Again, remember that not all invitations to connect are beneficial for your personal and professional objectives. It can be tempting to accept all invites, but scrutiny pays off, especially if you want to keep your network rich and fruitful.

Twitter as a message channel:

Twitter is a "messaging service" in which participants send short 140-character emails. Twitter messages are easy to read quickly, and the service has developed wide appeal. You may link images and web links to extend your messages. Twitter is great as a professional tool, but your messages may easily get lost in the noise of many competing messages.

Recently Twitter has been adding advertising, hashtags, trending topics, and embeddable posts, so that the service may increase income from advertising. Also, Twitter purchased Vine, an application that lets its users create six-second videos. How these changes affect Twitter's usefulness for the professional artist is still not clear. But, once again, watch how things develop carefully.

Twitter works better if you use it often. But unless the content is rich, your followers will wither away. I have about fifty followers, but I usually "tweet" only when I send out a new email or a new blog post. (This is an automatic option with MailChimp (http://www.mailchimp.com) (discussed in a later chapter). Unfortunately I have never seen anything useful to me come from Twitter.

Facebook as a message channel:

Facebook and its professional cousin, the Facebook Fan Page, may be useful to the professional artist. However, Facebook was built to encourage personal communications among friends, not professional clients.

Also, Facebook is continually changing. By company policy, once a week a new version is launched. Most times the changes are small but subtle. But sometimes there are unannounced big changes.

Many of these changes occur to boost Facebook's income by making advertisements more attractive to their sponsors. Recently Facebook has added embedded posts and trending topics from various newsfeeds that will show up on your Facebook news page. These items are intermixed advertisements and with any postings by you or your readers. Facebook's goal is to encourage discussion of advertisers' stories.

For you, as a professional artist who is marketing your artwork, these changes may not always be in your favor. Watch the situation with care. Facebook's usefulness for the professional artist is still not clear.

Always take care not to mix personal communications on your Facebook page with communications on your professional Fan Page. This is not easy, as sometimes things mix automatically. Again, the issue is to always watch your professional image.

Also, anything you post on your personal page may be found again on Facebook forever after, and will probably be mixed with your professional page. Even items that Facebook itself has destroyed sometimes come back. Always be careful about what you post.

I only use Facebook to communicate with my grandchildren. I have a professional presences on Facebook Fan Pages- as an artist and as an author, but I give them little attention.

Google+ as a message channel:

Unlike Facebook, Google+ pages and posts may help you reach people beyond a social network. Google+'s integration with various Google products and technologies, including Google Search and YouTube, makes it an interesting business tool.

Unlike blogging, email, and tweeting, on Google+ you say what you have to say, and then decide whom you are going to send it to. [17] Google+ is growing, but you may find that your prospective collector has yet to find this path. It is a path that requires watching as to its usefulness.

Pinterest as a message channel:

Pinterest is a visual social network that allows users to pin images, organize those images into collages called "pinboards," and share these images and pinboards with others. [18]

Each image may have a description of your artwork, the price, and a link to your website. This data travels with the image, even as it is repinned by others to another user's pinboards. Any correctly identified pin may expose users to your artwork images and drive them directly to your website. [19]

Pinterest recently launched business accounts, which allow more links and routes to your website. [20]

I have mixed feelings about the value of Pinterest to the professional artist. But it can hardly be neglected. Pinterest has more than seventy million registered users, [21] mostly women, who are reported as spending more money than visitors to all other social media sites. [22] I have my images posted on Pinterest, but I have yet to see any benefit.

Instagram as a messaging channel:

Instagram is a social discovery channel, not a visual blog. It is not clear if this is a worthwhile channel for the professional artist. Users are constantly searching for new content, mostly by using hashtags. Instagram is useful in showing your artistic culture, which is usually not a goal for marketing artworks. [23] So far I have not used it.

Other social media messaging channels:

There are many others. Some may present attractive ways of driving interest in your website. Some are growing fast. Most are not yet proven to help you develop serious prospects. All must be watched.

Summary:
1. Outbound marketing involves marshaling many message channels to promote your brand and to provide details about you and your artwork.
2. Not all messaging channels are equally useful. Some, such as email and your website, communicate directly with your prospective collectors and have power and importance. Others are sometimes confusing or labor-intensive.
3. Social media message channels are fluid and frequently changing. They require attention because they offer hazards and opportunities.

Here is where to start: With help from later chapters, master email and your website. Learn all you can about the other outbound message channels. Watch them carefully for opportunities. Manage your time carefully.

3. INBOUND MARKETING

Inbound Marketing:

When you swing open the doors to your art exhibit, you are hoping that your promotions, advertising, and mailings are going to bring prospective collectors to your door to meet you and to discuss and (hopefully) buy your artwork.

Inbound marketing is somewhat similar. It is a rapidly changing area of marketing, where the outbound communication channels that you have set up (as discussed in the previous chapter) will encourage your prospective collectors to come to you, often by email, or more likely via your website.

A recent survey indicates that 83 percent of adult Americans use the Internet. [24] You may expect that the statistics for prospective collectors are at least similar, and are likely much higher. Prospective collectors may expect you to solicit them using the Internet. And you should expect them to respond the same way.

The web page where your prospect arrives at your website is called the "landing page." It is the most important page of your website. Landing pages and their design are discussed in great detail in a later chapter.

Welcoming your prospective collector:

Your outbound channels have been used to send messages to selected, interested, and permissive prospective collectors who want to hear or read more about you and your artwork. Inbound marketing is about being ready to handle these inquires.

Become comfortable with giving away information. Inbound marketing relies on your willingness to tell your prospects everything they want to know about you, your artwork, how it is created, and how it is marketed. With inbound marketing, you are a sales guide whose mission is to help your prospective collector decide to become a customer.

Many artists find this a difficult role. But as a professional artist you will have to do some selling if you are going to make a living from your artwork. [25]

You must have answers for all stages of the buying process, and you must continue to delight your prospective collectors, so that they will continue to buy from you in the future. Do this, and the chances are that they will tell their friends and colleagues to buy from you too. [26]

With your help, your prospective collectors are going to take a journey:
1. They will arrive as your website visitor, via a phone call or email, or at a face-to-face meeting with you at an art show. Make them welcome.
2. Introduce them to your artwork.
3. Convert them to becoming a subscriber to your email list.
4. Warm them up about your artwork. As they begin to really like it, they become potential buyers.
5. Encourage them to fall in love with a particular artwork piece. Now there is an opportunity to close the sale. (There are more details on closing in a later chapter).

6. Close the sale, and they have become a collector of your artwork. [27]

This is the "buying cycle." For high-priced products such as many artworks, this cycle (seduction) may last a long time: days, weeks, or even months.

Gathering data about your prospects:

When you are interfacing with your prospective collectors, always remember to record data for future discussions. Here are two tools that may be helpful. Frankly, though, I prefer a piece of paper to take notes.

Evernote Hello (http://www.evernote.com/hello) is a free application for your smartphone. Evernote Hello creates a profile of your prospect. With the application you may connect with LinkedIn, connect to Facebook, or manually create a profile.

When first using the application, you enter your basic data. Then you may:
1. Type in the details yourself
2. Pass your smartphone to your prospects to type in their own data
3. Use the feature "Hello Contact" to automatically enter data from other nearby Evernote Hello users.

If you have a tablet, another application is Chimpadeedoo (http://www.mailchimp.com/features/mobile-signup-forms). It is useful to collect prospect data and automatically enter it into your MailChimp email prospect list. This is discussed in more detail in a later chapter.

*How will your prospective collector find you?*ß

How will they find you if they are not on your email list? Many people, collectors included, use the major Internet search engines—Google, Bing, and Yahoo—to find answers to their questions.

As an example, using these engines, type in your name, "Joe Blow, artist," and see how easy it is to find you. The more you use your outgoing messaging channels, the better the search engines will know where to find you.

It is not easy to be at the top of the search pile. In a later chapter there is a discussion on using keywords (sometimes called tags). They help get your website toward the top of the search results.

Referrals:

Referrals are another great inbound marketing channel. To get a referral, define to yourself your ideal collector. What makes them amazing?

Identify the best referrers among your collectors. These people already think highly of your work. Then, work to educate them with what makes you unique (branding, again). Give them content to share with other potential collectors. Always ask for referrals.

After you have received a referral, always recognize your referrers with a thank-you note.

Once again, always make a professional impression. If on your way you receive negative comments, do not pass over or delete them. Use them as an opportunity to respond with a positive viewpoint.

Remember that today, when marketing, keep using continuous engagement (inbound) as well as campaign (outbound) approaches.

Summary:

1. Inbound marketing is handling the contacts from prospective collectors and encouraging them to continue the process.
2. Understand the buying cycle, and help your prospect along the path.
3. Have patience.

Here is where to start: Recognize what is going on when a prospect contacts you. Welcome the contact. Make it easy for the prospect to get to know you and your artwork.

4. WRITING CONTENT

When enticing a prospective collector to respond to your outbound marketing channels, the content of your message is key. It is easy for a recipient to ignore or delete your message. You have to hook the reader from the very first word.

"Your readers have a low tolerance for boredom. The constant availability of competitive, entertaining attractions will always be pulling at them. Your ability to gain and hold their attention depends entirely upon your success in stimulating their curiosity." –Roy H. Williams

Content creation isn't as simple as stringing together a few words and clicking "publish." To hold the attention of the reader, the content must be interesting, entertaining, and easy to read.

"The attention span of the reader is not relevant, it is the quality of what they are reading." –Jerry Seinfeld

Bad content writing comes from:
1. Ignorance on your part of who your prospective collector is.
2. Bypassing your prospective collector by omitting empathy with them in your writing.

3. Using clichés and therefore showing a lack of original thinking.
4. A total lack of writing craft.

In a similar way, trying to convince your prospective collector by using logic is tough: as they read, they are arguing with you in their head. If you do succeed, it is only on an intellectual basis. Prospective collectors will not be inspired by reason alone. [28]

Storytelling:

"But," you say, "writing about me and my artworks is boring!" This is an excuse. Storytelling works better than any logic, and it is never boring. [29] [30]

You may be writing about your artworks, but that doesn't mean you can't weave in a little storytelling. Telling stories or anecdotes is a great way to engage your prospective collectors and make your content relatable. It also makes prospective collectors realize that behind that stuffy, shy artist is a real person who is full of interesting information.

Don't be afraid to draw from your personal experiences—just be sure they relate back and transition well to the topic of your content. Tell stories about how you created each artwork. Talk about what inspires you. Explain how you made choices as you developed the artwork.

Make your readers smile. This one is a little tougher, as it requires a sense of humor. You don't have to be the funniest person in the world to make your prospective collectors smile here and there. Sometimes your choice of words, or a little parenthetical quip, will do the trick. Just loosen up and be yourself. If you're not sure whether something is actually humorous, run it by someone else for an outside opinion.

Have confidence:

The best stories are simple. Have the confidence to say what you need to say, and then stop. Great writing and speaking in marketing come from confidence. You know what you are talking about and passionately believe it is important and true. No matter what the content of your message is, writing it with confidence guarantees it will be well received.

Confidence tells your prospective collectors that they are in good hands with you and your brand. It tells them that they will be going on a journey that you want them to go on. The journey may not be pleasant, but it is an intended journey, led by an expert guide.

Prospective collectors want to be led by an expert storyteller. Messages or stories that lack confidence quickly lose them. If you combine confidence with a smart, compelling story, you are on track to a successful communication.

Unfortunately, much marketing content lacks confidence, even if it is careful, professional, and intelligent. It tends to be bland, muddy, and boring. You may be full of self-confidence and passion about what you are writing about. But maybe your confidence does not come through in your writing and speaking.

Perhaps you fear that you will be laughed at or not taken seriously if you show that you really care about your message. Maybe you are not used to to writing or talking with passion.

Insecure people fill every pause with babble. They fill every bit of white space with talk about benefits.

If you do not really believe in your story, you will feel compelled to dress it up with jargon. However, if you believe in what you are writing or talking about, you will just say what you mean. Confident marketing uses plain language.

Have fun when you write. You are not in high school detention! Confident content is fun to create.

I found that a great way to become a better speaker and writer is to join a local group of Toastmasters International. (http://www.toastmasters.org) I was a member for a number of years and gained greatly from the experience.

Write and speak with passion and empathy:

Have passion. Believe that what you write and speak really matters. After all, you are writing or talking about your artwork. You created it. If you are writing or talking about something else and it does not matter, do not write or talk about it! If it does matter, write or talk about it with passion. Share your sincere conviction.

It is the same if you are writing or talking about yourself. You are the artist who produced this great artwork. Describe how you created it. What feelings of doubt, inspiration, and pleasure did you have during the creative process?

Write for your prospective collector:

When writing or talking, focus on your targets, your prospective collectors. Ensure that they understand that every word is for them. Start with empathy, and communicate empathy early and often.

Expose your agenda. Marketing is something you do "with" your prospective collectors, not "to" them. Weak content comes across as slightly dishonest because it is not really comfortable with its marketing role. If you believe in your story, you want the reader to have it. This means that marketing to them is not a dirty thing, but a friendly one.

Say what you really, really "want" to say, instead of what you feel you "should" say. Say it with all the passion, belief, and confidence you have inside.

"If you cannot find any belief or passion or confidence inside about what you are writing or talking about, maybe you should not be a professional artist." David Kessler.

Friction:

There is a concept known as "friction" that has been around marketing theory for years. With modern communications it comes up frequently. Friction refers to bumps in the road that interrupt the flow of information to the recipient.

Suppose you are writing a paragraph and you come to a point at which you would like the reader to click on a link so that he may read or view some other document. You are interrupting the information flow to the reader.

The reader internalizes, "Should I click on this link?" or, "This has been pretty boring; here is an excuse to drop out and look at something else that may be more interesting."

If you have the readers hooked, they may flow past this "friction." Or you may lose them. It all depends upon the quality of your content. Friction always gives the reader a push toward dropping out.

Writing for the computer, tablet, or smartphone:

Writing good marketing copy is very difficult. Writing good copy to be read on a computer, tablet, or smartphone screen is even harder. Writing your next email, Twitter entry, blog, or page of your website requires great care and thought. (This is discussed in more detail in later chapters, particularly regarding emails and websites.)

Start with the subject line. Keep it short. Remember that many smartphones only show the first few words. Hook your reader with those first words. Make it compelling yet friendly, to keep the reader from dropping out.

Many readers will look at the first words of the first paragraph and will not scroll through the text that follows. With a smartphone, where the visible text is short, again it is important that you hook the reader with the first words of your message. Always ask yourself, "How much value is there in the rest of the text?" Make your message short.

Is the tone and terminology appropriate for a prospective collector? Avoid jargon. Teach but do not lecture. (My wife uses the term "finger wagging.") Tell stories. Use lots of empathy.

The call for action:

Do you have a "call for action?" That is, have you told the reader what action you want him to do as a result of reading or hearing your message? This is so often forgotten.

Even good content fizzles out once it has made its point. Great content earns the right to ask the reader to do something, but the call for action asks the reader to actually do it. Be sure to match your call for action to the needs of the reader.

Use links to take the reader to important supporting material. But remember, links introduce friction, and the majority of readers will not click through.

Some old-school but still important hints:

1. Be sure you use "you" instead of "I" in your writing and talking. With "you" the prospective collectors relate to themselves.
2. Use "collector" instead of "customer" or "buyer." This keeps you focused on who is important.
3. Be sure, when writing or talking, that you are answering the questions raised by your prospective collector, and not just answering questions you raised yourself. This is an easy trap to become caught in.
4. Carefully craft your "profile" and "about us" web pages wherever they occur. They are advertisements about you.

Your Elevator Pitch:

Develop an "elevator pitch," sometimes called a "value proposition." This is a very useful tool to memorize and have with you at all times. It gets its name from the idea that if you are getting into an elevator with your best prospective collector, how do you tell him everything about you and your artwork in the short interval between floors?

Once you develop an elevator pitch, you may use it whenever you meet someone and wish to tell them about yourself in just a few words. Your pitch takes time to evolve. But preparing it makes you focus on what is important.

My elevator pitch as an artist is, "I paint ordinary people, doing everyday things, at interesting places." I use it when I am talking to a prospective collector while standing by my painting at an art exhibit, and in a thousand other circumstances.

There are additional values in an elevator pitch:
1. It allows you to differentiate your artwork from others (part of your branding process).
2. It points out your strong values—what you are really good at.
3. It couples you to your artwork.
4. It will aid you when you are designing your website and your outbound messages.

A good elevator pitch takes time to mature. Do not expect to get there on your first attempt. My pitch has gradually changed over the years. Always think about it from your prospective collector's viewpoint. [31]

Some Last Thoughts:

Many artists hate such networking, but 90 percent of potential collectors value personal connections when talking, phoning, and in emails.

To be successful with content requires self-confidence, courage, focus, discipline, practice, and openness to change.

A good story captures your prospective collector's attention, and takes him on a brief journey as to how you came to create the artwork.

What is useful?
1. Don't pitch me if I have already read or downloaded the information.
2. Strengthen content that fits my interest.
3. Do not pitch existing collectors the same way.

Your prospective collector has the power to block out the interruptive messaging of traditional advertising channels. With the rise of social media, prospective collectors are more interested in starting a conversation than being spoken at. Social media provides a place where they may foster these desired conversations.

Prospective collectors will feel interrupted if you are just sending them spammy mass messages. If you are not providing them with quality content that their mom, friend, or coworker could have sent them, you are just another brand in the crowd.

Social media that is personalized, relevant, and engaging—the type of content that your personal connections produce—is the type of content that succeeds in inbound marketing. It's the type of content that gets shared. It's the type of content that helps generate leads. It's the type of content that delights your prospective collectors. [32]

Summary:

1. Always write to hold your prospect's attention from the first word.
2. Make your writing interesting, entertaining, and easy to read.
3. Watch out for friction.
4. Always use storytelling, confidence, passion, and empathy.
5. Use your elevator pitch.
6. Do not forget your call for action.

Here is where to start: Outline your elevator pitch. This will get your thoughts organized. Learn to write and talk about your messages as stories.

5. CLOSING THE SALE

Your outbound and inbound marketing has worked, and you have your prospective collector standing in front of you. You see "love in their eyes" for your artwork. It is time to close the sale. [33]

Many books have been written about "closing," but there is one method that works well with artwork: the "puppy dog" close. Take the artwork off the wall or stand, and put it into the loving arms of the prospective collector. He or she will find it hard to give it back! [34]

Price:

Closely related to closing is "price." Pricing the artwork is very subjective, and it greatly depends upon where you are.

If you are trying to sell at art festivals, and the majority of the artworks on show are craft, the prospective collectors passing by will expect your price to be low.

If you are selling at a B&M gallery, the prospective collector will expect the price to be in the range of other artworks sold by the gallery— possibly medium to high.

If you are selling at a New York gallery, the expectations are that the price will be high—maybe very high.

Another criterion is where you are in your career. The artworks of emerging artists tend to be priced lower than those of well-established artists.

Setting your prices requires lots of research:
1. Look at the prices of other artists who make artworks that are somewhat similar to your own.
2. Look at artists who are already where you aspire to be.
3. Judge yourself hard. Put yourself in the mind of your prospective collector, looking at all artists.

I price my paintings by the square inch. For paintings, this is the most common approach. It keeps things simple. I have a modestly sliding scale that slightly varies the price per inch depending upon the overall size of the painting. Small paintings have the largest per-square-inch price. For larger paintings, the price is somewhat lower.

Keep your emotional connection to the painting out of the pricing. Prospective collectors may not see your artwork in the same way that you do. Often I have been surprised by how others feel about my paintings. Paintings I love, go unloved. Others I think of as poor, are loved. It is hard to tell what others feel.

Be consistent in your pricing. Transparency in pricing is so important. The Internet lets everyone know your prices. It helps to have the same prices everywhere.

Occasionally you may wish to start a new body of work in a totally new style. This goes against the previous discussions about consistency. To do so requires you to be careful about pricing, as you may confuse your current collectors.

A new style may require a whole new pricing structure. Your previous pricing has possibly been set by years of exposure and market maturity. Start a new program of market research to see where you stand in this new marketplace.

Affordability:

On the other hand, even with consistency in pricing, discounts are sometimes possible. When negotiating, I might throw in the shipping costs or taxes. For a multiple sale to the same collector, I may give a "collector's discount" of 10 percent on the second or subsequent purchase in the same sale.

I find that price is rarely the issue in a sale. Usually the main concern from the buyer's viewpoint is affordability. When you have stated the price, what crosses the mind of many collectors is, "Can I afford that price?" They rarely question your valuation.

If this issue appears, it is time to negotiate—not necessarily on price, but consider such things as an affordable down payment and the balance spread out over time. I have used this repeatedly, and never had anyone default on payment. Meanwhile, they get to enjoy the painting they love.

Or maybe it is time to absorb shipping costs or taxes. Or try a rent-to-buy option. I have done this, and even had my painting returned in excellent condition after several months of income. There are a lot of alternatives to just lowering your listed price.

Of course, some collectors just like to deal. They enjoy the chase. Perhaps some of the discount paths might work.

Getting paid:

Your prospect is ready to buy. We have discussed taxes, packing, shipping, and method of payment. Make sure that this last step it is easy.

I have arranged through both PayPal (http://www.paypal.com) and Square (http://www.square.com) to take major credit cards. These services, upon request when setting up an account, will provide you with a free attachment that plugs into the headset socket of both your tablet and smartphone. Then, using a free downloaded application, you may securely and inexpensively accept credit card payments in your studio or at an art show or fair. PayPal and Square provide comprehensive free training videos and online instruction, all for a very low percentage of the sale price.

Generally I will not take checks (unless I really know the buyer), especially certified checks, as there is too much fraud associated with them.

Summary:

1. You do not get paid unless you close the sale—the "puppy dog" close.
2. Setting pricing is subjective. It is driven by knowing your marketplace.
3. Keep the transaction transparent and consistent.
4. Affordability: use discounts, terms, make it easy.
5. Getting paid is helped by Square and Paypal.

Here is where to start: Learn how to close at the end of the buying cycle. Think through your pricing structure and price point.

6. YOUR COMPUTER

As I discussed earlier, email is today's preferred method of communication. In the same way, a web page is the expected point of contact for inbound marketing. Also, social media channels are becoming increasingly important as part of an artist's marketing toolbox.

Today a professional artist needs to have, at the very least, modest computer skills. Even if you have an assistant or a significant other to help, you will be crippled without today's tools of the trade at your fingertips: a fairly powerful computer with lots of memory, a large display, a smartphone, and a tablet.

Computer hardware:

Like social media, computer hardware, displays, software, smartphones, tablets, and all other accessories are continually being updated. In general, it is not necessary to have the latest of everything. But often there are real improvements with later models that will make life easier for you.

I have an Apple computer in my office. The front-end costs are a little higher, but everything easily integrates together. The quality of the product is first class, and the warranties and after-sale support are wonderful.

I have a large-screen Apple iMac with lots (20 GB) of RAM (internal memory), two additional large external storage disk drives, an iPad, and an iPhone. Plus, I have a second, older Mac system in my studio by my easel. This second system is used just to display reference images as I paint. This computer is spattered with paint from being accidentally poked with wet brushes or my fingers when I am concentrating on some detail on the canvas. This computer is connected by Wi-Fi to my main iMac so that I can transfer image files.

Accessory hardware and services:

You need a moderately high-speed Internet service. This is a requirement if you send quality images to prospective collectors, vendors (such as printing services), or B&M and online galleries. The Internet connection can be via cable or DSL (which tends to be much slower) services, usually through a special modem in or near your studio. Some parts of the country have inexpensive, very high-speed service through fiber-optic cables. If you have this, I envy you.

Your incoming service modem is usually connected to a wireless router that, in turn, transmits a Wi-Fi signal throughout your studio and office area, providing connections to your computers, smartphone, and tablet.

As you collect digital versions of artwork and reference images, you will need lots of digital storage, usually in the form of external hard disk drives. Quality image files, as discussed later, can be very big. Multiple large-capacity disk drives may be needed. Fortunately, as I buy more, they always seem to get less expensive.

Since these digital image records are valuable to your business, and computer hardware is always vulnerable to crashes and failures, you must plan for data backups. This involves storing digital duplicates of your valuable records both locally and at an off-site storage service.

Hard disk drives, today's standard for recording computer records, have a limited life and will fail. Even CDs and DVDs become unreadable after a few years of sitting on a shelf.

I have two large (1 TB each) backup storage hard disk drives close to my computer. With these I use an Apple automatic minute-to-minute backup system called Time Machine (http://www.apple.com/support/timemachine). Similar backup processes are available for other brands of computer systems.

In addition, I utilize an outside service, Backblaze (http://www.backblaze.com), which every night duplicates any changes to my computer records from the previous night and sends the data to an off-site location. Using either of these resources, in the event of a failure or catastrophe, I am able to recover my valuable records. Other similar off-site backup services are available, but I am only familiar with this one.

Another important accessory is a printer. I use two: a very high-quality ink-jet color printer, and a low-cost black-and-white laser printer. The latter prints on both sides of the paper when required. Most of my printing is done using the laser printer on ordinary paper.

In general, printers are priced low, but their replaceable ink cartridges are expensive. My high-quality color printer is fitted with an add-on "continuous flow" ink feed system. [35] The colored ink flows from bottles directly to the print heads. The continuous flow system does away with ink cartridges. Bottled ink is relatively cheap.

I use the color printer to make such things as high-quality art prints and promotional art note cards, all on quality paper. I am able to print most of my promotional materials.

To create high-quality images of my artwork, I use a flatbed scanner. This process is described in detail in an article on my website [36], and the subject is discussed more in a later chapter.

Software:

There are certain computer software programs that I have found to be very useful:

Adobe Photoshop Elements. (http://www.adobe.com/products/photoshop-elements.html) This is the little brother of the well-known industrial-level Adobe Photoshop software used at many design studios. I use it to repair small flaws in my photographed and scanned images; to resize, crop, and compress images; and to knit together images as part of my painting scanning process. All this is discussed in more detail in a later chapter. *Evernote.* (http://www.evernote.com) This is a wonderful tool—actually a family of products—that you will love after you have used it for a while. Evernote makes modern office life manageable by letting you easily collect and find everything that matters. You may gather all your notes, ideas, images, and tasks into one place. And unless you want certain extra features, it is free. Be sure to sign up for their blog.

I used Evernote to help me put this book together.

Summary:
1. You will need a fairly powerful, reasonably modern computer, a fairly big computer screen, lots of digital storage, an off-site backup service, a printer, and possibly a scanner.
2. Backup and image processing software are very important.
3. A smartphone and tablet are very helpful.
4. A fast Internet connection is important.

Here is where to start: If you are not a computer whiz, find someone who is. You are going to need him or her. Contract with a reliable off-site backup service. Use it. Your computer system will break, and you will need to recover your files.

7. WORKING WITH IMAGES

For you, as an artist, images have great importance. You work with images to use as references, and with images of your finished artworks. This chapter discusses taking, manipulating, and managing images of all kinds.

Reference images:

I use photographs, always taken by me, as references for my paintings. After selection and some manipulation, they are displayed on a computer screen beside my easel and provide guidance to my painting.

Over the years I have purchased various point-and-shoot cameras. I have always favored cameras with long focal length zoom lenses and with built-in systems that automatically stabilize the image—that is, taking out any shaking when capturing the image. Also, I like the camera to be small enough to hold in my hand and slip into my pocket. Since I like taking images of people in motion, I frequently use a burst mode, where a string of images are captured over just a few seconds.

Another criterion is the length of time between pressing the shoot button to when the camera actually takes the photograph. This has to do with the processing speed of the microchips in the camera. This time has to be short, or the scene you are trying to capture will have changed. Similarly, consider how long it takes from when you turn on the camera to when you may take the first picture.

All these features are available and optimized in many high-end, expensive cameras. A limited budget forces me to make some compromises when purchasing each camera. But again, as the years have gone by, more features are available for the same amount of money.

Since acquiring an iPhone, I have found that its small size and photo-taking convenience suits many of my needs. However, I still use my point-and-shoot camera with its zoom when looking for views and at people far away.

I take many photographs, frequently arriving back from even a short trip with hundreds of images. My collection now extends to many, many thousands of images. To manage all of these, I organize them into collections, labeled by the occasion or trip where they were taken.

A long time ago, long before Apple's iPhoto application was available, I began using another computer application, iView Media Pro. This company was later acquired by Microsoft and the application was renamed as Microsoft Expressions Media 2. Recently it was sold again, and the application became Phase One Media Pro. (http://www.phaseone.com/Downloads/Media-Pro-1.aspx) All of these applications operate similarly, with the biggest improvement over the years being an increased ability to sort and retrieve needed images.

Capturing artwork images:

I have images of nearly all of my artwork, going back to when I began serious painting. Initially I shot the images myself, using my point-and-shoot camera. I made all the usual errors: not centered, skewed, pinched, bloated, reflections, focus issues, and lighting and color problems. Many of these issues led to difficulties when I tried to crop the image to remove the frame or the paper/canvas edge.

Quality images of your artwork are essential for the professional artist. The images are needed for personal record-keeping, for many marketing channels, and for a secondary income channel (professional prints).

The quality of the artwork image is determined by how the original image is captured: the resolution of the camera, the accuracy of the original shot, the lighting, and the color accuracy.

For documenting my artwork, I quickly turned to a local professional photographer. He had a very high-grade camera and professional lighting systems, and could return to me a CD with my painting image nicely captured, color-corrected, and ready to use.

These photographers often have a special lighting arrangement to handle three-dimensional artwork. Also, such artwork will often require multiple image views to record each piece.

Later I developed another method of capturing images of my paintings, using my 8.5 x 14-inch color scanner.

To make use of the scanner, I use the inexpensive computer application Adobe Photoshop Elements, which I mentioned in the last chapter. The application is updated every year or so, but the basic editing tools remain much the same. This layman's version of the expensive professional-grade Adobe Photoshop application is all that most artists will ever need.

Photoshop Elements has a feature called "Panorama." This allows the stitching together of multiple photographs to form a very large image. I have developed a method of scanning my paintings in small strips, and I then use the software to make a large, high-resolution image of the entire painting. The process works for paintings up to about 24 x 48 inches. This process is described in detail in an article on my website. [36]

Digital images:

Today, digital techniques are used almost exclusively in artwork recordkeeping. I still have many 4 x 5-inch transparencies and 35 mm color slides of my earlier work, however. Most of these older records have been scanned and converted into their digital equivalents.

For most purposes, a digital resolution of 300 DPI (dots per inch) measured on the surface of the artwork is adequate.

Dots per inch goes back to the days when photographs were reproduced in newspapers and magazines. Ordinary newspapers could get away with 100 to 150 printed dots per inch for a black-and-white image. High-grade color magazine images required closer to 300 DPI. This term still is used when referring to ink-jet printers, since they actually lay down dots of pigment.

Today, the reference to printed dots for images has been replaced by the term *pixels.* This arises from the use of computer screen images. Each dot has become a pixel.

A 300 DPI resolution means that a 16 x 20-inch painting has 4,800 x 6,000 pixels. The entire image has 28,800,000 pixels (nearly 29 megapixels). This is still far beyond the resolution of today's low-cost point-and-shoot cameras, though technical advancements are changing the rules frequently.

Artwork records management:

I manage my artwork data in several ways. All of my paintings, going back almost to my early ones, have a serial number. One day, long after I had started painting, I realized this was important, so I started a list. I went through my storage area and numbered all of my paintings at random. From that time on, each new painting has been added to the list. Of course I missed a few at the time of the original list, and those are now numbered 0-1, 0-2, etc.

To keep records of these numbers and related data for each painting, after trying many record-keeping applications, I now happily use Arawak's Flick! (http://www.arawak.com.au/flick.html) For each painting I record a small image and its size, serial number, and availability, plus details of where it has been exhibited, price, sales and buyer's details, etc.

Artwork titles:

It is appropriate here to talk about artwork titles. Many artists are, in my opinion, lazy and just label some of their artwork "Untitled." Do you really think that any collector is going to get serious about owning a painting named "Untitled 23"?

Apart from the difficulty of record-keeping, such a title is totally uninspiring to a collector. Just name your artwork anything: "A Thought Before Breakfast," "Life on a Tuesday Morning"—the words do not actually have to mean anything, but the name makes that artwork unique to you.

For a long time it was conventional to insert underlines between words of artwork titles for a computer record. Google recently changed their data-scanning algorithm. They now state that with underlines they look at each word individually. To record titles as a block, they now require hyphens between words. For example, you should write your artwork titles for your website as "A-Thought-Before-Breakfast" if you wish Google to read the title as a whole into their records.

Artwork computer records:

My artwork images are organized on my office computer in a single large computer file called "Artwork Collections." Within this file I created many separate subfiles, one for each piece of artwork. Each subfile appears alphabetically and is named "(Title) Collection." "Title" is the name of the piece of artwork.

Into this file goes a copy of every computer file that is related to that painting: artwork files in assorted resolutions, text files with descriptions of the artwork used for marketing projects, files for printing art cards of that artwork in various sizes, etc.

The suffixes .tiff, .raw, and .jpg appear after a computer image file name and describe the technical nature of the file. In RAW and most TIFF files the data is uncompressed, while JPG (or sometimes written "JPEG") files are compressed to reduce the file size. Compressing a computer file always loses some details of that image. But making the file smaller makes storage and handling easier.

For each artwork image, I always make a range of resized computer files, each stored in the "(title) collection" file:

1. The original scanned or photographed computer file at its maximum, uncompressed size, if possible as a TIFF (or more recently as a RAW data file). This "master" file

contains all the data that has been captured about the artwork image. This file may be very large.

2. A JPG compressed version of this file. This file is smaller than the original "master" file, but often still quite large.

3. A reduced-resolution compressed JPG version of the master file, compressed to just less than 30 megabytes. (Note the difference between pixels and megabytes. Pixels determine the physical image size. Megabytes is a measure of the stored size of the computer file containing that image. They are related, but not exactly.) This reduced-size computer file is specified by several services that may provide quality art prints of your artwork. This is discussed in more detail below.

4. A reduced-resolution compressed JPG version of the master file, compressed to just less than 25 megabytes. This size file is specified by several other services that provide art prints of your artwork.

5. A reduced-resolution compressed JPG version of the master file, compressed to just less than 15 megabytes. This size file is specified by another group of services that provide art prints of your artwork.

6. A reduced-resolution compressed JPG version of the master file, compressed so that the longest image edge is reduced to 6 inches, with a resolution of 300 DPI. This file is popular for accompanying press releases incorporating the image.

7. An 800-pixel-wide JPG image for web use.
   (web images are forced by the process to have less color information than the high-quality images you have collected. [37] Photoshop Elements and similar software enable you to save files with automatically adjusted color quality to match web requirements.)

8. A similar 600-pixel-width web-quality image.
9. A similar 150-pixel high web-quality image.
10. A cropped 50 x 50-pixel web-quality image for use as a thumbnail button in my web page layout.

Color presentation of captured images is complicated. If the image is to be printed, the printing process uses colored inks and the paper often has surface texture and a slight coloration, all of which may affect the end result.

If the image is to be displayed electronically on a computer screen, a tablet, or a smartphone, the screen itself or the electronics behind it may distort the color. For precise color matching, the computer screen has to be calibrated to ensure the displayed result is close to true. [38]

When viewed from a website, the image will always have color shifts due to built-in color compression processes. For many practical situations, the viewer cannot compare with or has never seen the original artwork, and will not notice minor color shifts.

Using images for other sources of income:

In addition to selling original artworks, many artists, like photographers, may collect revenue by selling prints of their artwork images.

There is a wide range of possibilities: making prints yourself for sale, getting others to prepare and maybe market prints from your images, licensing your images to organizations that may use them for illustrations and book covers, your image on T-shirts and cell phone cases, etc. For many of these channels, you have to do little more than upload your image to the organization's website. I have used all these channels, to some profit.

To make prints yourself requires investment in a good-quality color printer and some skills and knowledge in paper and printing. I invested in such a high-end color printer, but recently found it easier and cheaper to use some of the very good online printing services.

These days I use my color printer primarily to make various promotional materials, including blank art note cards, sometimes with promotional text or thank-you notes printed on the inside.

Several years ago there was a lot of discussion about what was called "Giclee printing." Giclee was the name of a specific brand of high-end color printing. But the name has become generic to describe many custom high-end color printing services.

The general idea is that you have a few individually numbered, high-end prints manufactured, and that you market them yourself. The print looked very close to the original and might command a price that was less than the original, but still attractive to both the artist and the collector. Some artists have done very well at this.

For many artists, the downside was that you had to purchase several of these prints in advance to obtain a good price from the printer, and then hold an inventory of them yourself, until they were sold.

To some extent, like the book industry, this market has been undermined by print-on-demand services. Today, an artist may obtain, from any of several suppliers, very high-quality prints, one at a time, for comparatively low prices. Moreover, the printer will prepare, mount, frame, and deliver this high-quality print to your order, for a very reasonable price.

If you wish, the printer will let you open a personal online store in your name, where your collectors may go to order these prints in a wide variety of sizes, finishes, and surfaces, matted and framed to the buyer's specifications. You receive an agreed-upon commission on prices that you set.

Such printers include ImageKind (http://www.imagekind.com) and FineArtAmerica. (http://www.fineartamerica.com)

At the other end of the range, several organizations will imprint your image upon any of a hundred or more gift or craft items. Again, you receive a commission on sales. Such printers include Zazzle (http://www.zazzle.com) and RedBubble (http://www.redbubble.com).

For some years I have received a small income from these services.

In addition, several companies have approached me to license my images for book and magazine covers and illustrations. These deals are all individual and negotiated depending upon expected distribution or circulation. In each case the company found the images on my website.

Copyright issues:

Some artists are concerned about copyright issues and their images. My large, high-quality files are safely on my computer and are not distributed except to individual printers, where they are closely guarded. The images that appear in my emails or on my and others' websites are of small size and low resolution. Any copies from these sources would be of very poor quality.

Someone could always paint a copy of any of my paintings. But then, the saying is that "copying is the greatest form of flattery!" However, to avoid copyright issues, I always use my own photography for reference images.

If you want to keep tabs on your artwork images, see what people are pinning on Pinterest (http://pinterest.com/source/YourwebsiteURL). Also, do a reverse image search of your JPEG art images. You can do a reverse image search using the application TinEye (http://www.tineye.com).

If you find that your art was used by others without your permission, here are some organizations that can help:

1. Creative America: United Against Content Theft (http://www.creativeamerica.org)
2. Defend Art (http://www.defendart.org)
3. Legal Art (http://www.legalart.biz)

Summary:

1. Managing your images: use reference images along with your artwork images.
2. Understand the various types and sizes of digital image.
3. Manage your artwork records.
4. Get income from prints and other uses of your images.
5. Be aware of possible copyright issues.

Here is where to start: Ensure that you have a method of making quality images of all your artwork. Establish an image management plan.

8. USING EMAIL

Today, email is the preferred tool for professional communication. It is what I use for most of my communications.

Snail mail has its place, but it is not as convenient or even practical for today's high-speed, day-to-day or even minute-to-minute communications.

Also, if needed, email communications may be directed to multiple recipients and may include attachments such as images and documents.

There is nothing worse than sending an email to a prospective collector and not having it read. Many things may interfere with the email's successful delivery and getting it read. [39] [40] Some of these issues and their solutions are explored below.

Getting your email read—those first few words:

A basic email message consists of a subject line followed by text. Today, 70 percent or more of businesspeople receive emails on a smartphone that has a small screen. My own email reports show that 72 percent of my prospective collectors are using smartphones. Unlike displays on a desktop screen or tablet, on a smartphone it is only possible to see the first few words of your subject line, and the first two or three lines of your message.

Since your purpose in sending emails is to have your email opened and read, this makes the design of the front end of your email message critical.

As I've discussed earlier, competition from other messages always awaits your recipient's attention. This makes it easy for your message to be skipped or deleted in favor of something more attractive.

On a smartphone or tablet, even the need to tap the screen to open and read an email message presents "friction."

Crafting your email:

It is necessary to carefully craft the content (as discussed in an earlier chapter) as well as the layout of a marketing email.

There are a number of free tools that help create attractive outgoing email messages. I have used with great success the service MailChimp. (http://www.mailchimp.com) (Other similar services are available. But this is the one with which I am most familiar.)

With MailChimp you can build and manage your email lists, design each email message (they call each message a "campaign"), and analyze your results after the mailing. MailChimp provides many useful training videos and an informative blog. (If you use their service, I recommend that you subscribe to the blog.)

How your email is displayed:

How you prepare your email message may have significant effects on how it is displayed. If you prepare the message using a word processor, unseen characters may be inserted. Also, when the message is displayed, the line length may be predetermined and not flow according to the size of the recipient's display. This could be a particular problem when your message is received by a smartphone.

MailChimp has developed message layout templates that use "responsive design." These adjust the text and images according the size of the screen upon which the email is displayed. This subject is explored in more detail in the next chapter.

Crafting content:

Your recipients expect your email to be relevant to their interests. [41] To begin with, get personal. Use the reader's first name.

When you accumulated your lists of prospects, as discussed below, you likely recorded the first and last name for each, as well as the email address. MailChimp has a simple tag that automatically picks out the first name for each recipient and inserts it at the front of the email.

Your message stands out, even on a smartphone, because the recipients see their name.

(By the way, you may do the same with Twitter. Use "Hi Twittername.") [42]

The first five or so words of the subject line of your email are usually bolded on the smartphone display and stand out when viewed by your recipient. Ensure that these first words reflect the purpose of your attractive message. For maximum chance of opening, do the obvious: use the subject line to accurately describe the subject of your message! [43]

In the same way, the first fifteen or so words of your message (including your first-name greeting) may be seen on the smartphone screen. Make sure these words contain a compelling reason for the reader to open this message.

There is an old concept that goes back to the days of laying out newspaper pages: put your important news "above the fold." The idea was that newspapers were usually folded when shown for sale on a newsstand, and the headlines and stories that appeared above the fold were available for the prospective purchaser to see before buying.

The same idea applies to text on a computer screen and especially on a smartphone screen. To scroll down the screen requires effort and introduces "friction." Often the lower part of your message may not even be read.

Hook the reader quickly. Put the interesting part of your message at the top. Try to hold the attention of the reader so that he or she will overcome the scrolling friction and be encouraged to read down the page to see the rest of your message.

Remember that what interests you may not turn on your prospective collector reader. Put yourself in his shoes. Ask yourself, "Why would he want to read this?" Avoid spam and self-promotion. Be a storyteller; make your message interesting enough to hold the reader's attention against a background of competing interests.

Okay. You have made a good pitch. So what?:

There must be a purpose for your message. A man I worked for years ago always asked me, "How did I want the reader/listener to be different after receiving my message?" And even more important, "Why did I want them to be this way?"

As discussed in an earlier chapter, now is the time for a "call for action." All marketing messages should include a call for action, such as the following: get them to pick up the phone, fill out a form and give or send it to you, or click on a link or a button. Get them to do something that will inch them along the path to becoming a prospective collector, or maybe eventually buying one of your artworks.

Building lists:

An email message is not of much value without someone to send it to. When you start putting together an email list of prospective collectors, be sure that they have given you permission to send your messages (such as your newsletter). As was discussed in the outbound marketing chapter, this is today's permissive requirement when soliciting your prospective collectors.

Before adding people to my email list, I always ask them if they want to be included. When getting prospects to sign up at a show, I add a bold note to the top of the list: "Please sign up for my occasional newsletter." In other cases, I may send each new prospect an email, asking if he or she wishes to be added to my list.

In Europe and many other parts of the world, the rules are much tighter than here in the United States. Without this permission, your mailing is regarded as spam and may automatically be blocked.

When you add a name to a MailChimp list, MailChimp requests that you check a box signifying that you have permission to add that name.

Attachments:

Often you want the reader to click on a link to an image or a document. All email software applications have a way of adding attachments to a message. But friction problems can occur when viewing these attachments on a smartphone or tablet. Often the image or text is too big for the small screen.

PDF and MS Word documents are particularly troublesome. Adobe Reader, or a similar application, must be launched to read the document. On a smartphone the attachment is nearly impossible to read. Often the only solution is to print out the document. Frequently this is not convenient.

It is better that the attachment message text be merged into the main message, below the fold. The text will flow and adjust in size to be read on the small screen. MailChimp has layouts that allow you to insert images into the email text. Moreover, when the images are received from MailChimp, they are automatically resized to fit the display screen.

Continually think of possible friction issues. Make it easy for your prospective collector. Remember that the competition is always there, competing for his attention. Deliver the message, but keep it short.

Summary:

1. The first few words are the most important in both the subject line and message.
2. Emailing services like MailChimp are very helpful and are often free to use.
3. Get personal fast. Remember who you are talking to.
4. Include a call for action.
5. Build your list of permissive prospective collectors.

Here is where you start: Sign up for MailChimp—it is free. Watch the introductory videos. Practice writing short subjects and content. Start building your list of permissive prospective collectors.

9. YOUR WEBSITE

Your website is one of your most important marketing tools. It is your public "face." Your prospective collector comes to your website to learn, to browse or shop, and hopefully to buy.

Your website is the destination:
1. To view your artwork portfolio.
2. To find out how to contact you.
3. To obtain more information about you.
4. To find out how to purchase your artwork.

All of this data is spread out over a series of web pages, which collectively form your website. The various web pages are stored on a computer server owned or controlled by your website host.

Hosting:

Many organizations offer website hosting services. One of the most crucial decisions you make for your website is selecting your web host. It is essential to choose the right host or all of your hard work may be wasted, or even worse, lost.

Free web hosts are fine for playing around, but you will want something more for your business as a professional artist.

Questions to consider:
1. Do they provide an easy-to-use site building system? Most do, but many are proprietary and will only work on that host's servers, so that your site could not be moved if needed. I have had a very reputable host, whom I used for a long time, suddenly go out of business.
2. What is their reputation for uptime? That is, how often are they closed down for maintenance, making your website unavailable for your prospective collector to visit? Reputable hosts publish statistics of their uptime. Look for 99.99 percent or better.
3. Do not overbuy. Some hosts offer huge amounts of storage space for more money. Most likely your website will require only a modest amount of storage space, probably much less than 5GB.
4. Test the speed of your prospective host's network. (http://www.iwebtool.com/speed_test) Slow website response adds friction to your prospective visitor experience. But this issue overlaps with your website design. Too much data to be downloaded on a particular web page will also slow down the experience of your visitor. (This is discussed again later.)
5. Check out the quality of the host's customer service and help pages. Are they available 24-7 by toll-free telephone, as well as by email or online chat? Try calling them to see how they respond. Are you able to understand the person who answers?
6. If you want to do better for collecting payments than just using PayPal (http://www.paypal.com) or Square (http://www.square.com), do they offer a shopping cart system? What are their fees? [44]

I use a host called aPlus.net (http:/www.aplus.net), pay about $125 per year, and get great service.

Your Domain Name:

Your website has an address built around what is known as your *domain name.* Some less attractive website services use a name built around *their* domain name, with your name as a suffix. You see this frequently used for online shops, such as http://fineartamerica.com/peter-worsley.html.

As a professional, it is better to have your own distinctive domain name, such as http://www.peterworsley.com. Usually your host will help you purchase your domain name. Mine costs me ten dollars for a five-year renewal. Many names are already taken, but you can consider "peterworsleyart," "artofpeterworsley," or something similar. But keep it simple so that your prospective collectors can remember you.

When choosing a domain name, some things to consider:
1. Stick with a ".com" suffix. This will bring you credibility and trust. There are many other suffixes available, but everyone recognizes and feels comfortable with a .com address.
2. Find a name with only one spelling. People are poor spellers, and it will be easier for people to remember your domain.
3. The shorter, the better.
4. Make sure it has commercial appeal. Some names just do not work.
5. No hyphens, dots, or underlines. People forget to put them in.
6. Use your personal name if you can. Remember that you are the artist. Your name is important. [45]

MARKETING FOR PROFESSIONAL ARTISTS

Responsive Design:

As mentioned earlier, the majority of people today look at web pages and emails on smartphones and tablets. Your tech-savvy prospective collectors are likely to be using smartphones. My personal newsletter email list, using MailChimp, reports that 72 percent of my prospective collectors receive my messages on a small-screen smartphone.

Most smartphone and tablet users want to go directly from a link in an email message to a web page.

Another study [46] indicates that tablet users are important, spending 50 percent more at online retailers compared with smartphone users, and 20 percent more than traditional laptop or desktop users.

Older (traditionally designed) websites are built upon what are called "tables." The pieces of the web page are physically positioned, one piece related to another, in a matrix. When viewed on a smartphone, and often on a tablet, only a segment of the total web page is displayed. The user has to slide the page around to see the whole page. Or the website is just shrunk to fit the screen, and the images and text become unreadable

Because this introduces friction into the process of viewing the web page, newer approaches have evolved, known as "responsive design." The general idea is to assemble the displayed web page from a flowing stream of data, instead of from a preassembled matrix of data. The display layout may be adjusted as it is downloaded to suit the size of the screen.

To minimize viewer friction, today all professional web pages need to be designed or redesigned using responsive design.

In simplistic terms, with responsive design, upon receiving a request for a web page's data, the web host sends a message to the requester to find out what size screen the page data is going to be displayed upon. The stream of data then flows with transmitted images and text adjusted to match the screen width.

If the screen is wide enough, column breaks are inserted in the text stream, which allows the data to fill multiple columns across the receiving screen. On a small screen, the web page text and images fit the width of the screen, and the user simply scrolls down the page to see all the data.

Do not consider a new website design that does not incorporate a form of responsive design. If your existing website does not include this feature, it is time to think about an upgrade.

Landing page:

Most of your outgoing marketing messages encourage prospective collectors to visit your website. As briefly discussed in earlier chapters, the page where the prospect arrives at your website is called the landing page. It is the most important page of your website. From that point on, friction begins and, if not overcome by the design of the landing page, visitors begin to drop off and are lost.

Visitors who use the web have been trained to automatically tune out anything that is not immediately of interest. An attractive landing page has to have the following:

1. A header that grabs the visiting prospect within the first three seconds of landing. The rest of the page does not matter if the header does not meet the expectations of the reader.
2. Body copy that is interest-generating, to complement the header. It must talk about "why" more than "what."

3. Trust elements, such as an image of you at work in your studio, wording that may establish a comfort level in doing business with you, and maybe some testimonials from collectors. Most visiting prospects may have little or no real knowledge about you. Keep it short. Your visitor will be impatient.

4. Finally, calls for action to take the visitor where they want to go. Remember that this is the first friction step, and the visitor must already feel comfortable to move on.[47]

Often, but not always, the landing page is what is called the website's index page (usually http:/www.yourdomainname.com). There may be occasions when an artist has several distinct artwork lines: painting, illustrations, video, etc. Such an artist may wish to create several landing pages, one for each artwork line. Some artists even create separate websites for each artwork line.

As I stated in the opening paragraph, your visitors have come to the landing page because they want:

1. To view your artwork portfolio.
2. To find out how to contact you.
3. To obtain information about you.
4. To find out how to purchase your artwork.

Keep everything simple. Calls for action should be buttons or web links that take the visitor directly to these destinations.

You should add one more button or link to allow the visitor to sign up for your (newsletter) email list. MailChimp (http://www.mailchimp.com) provides some code that automatically generates such a signup form.

Your artwork portfolio:

This is where you show images, descriptions, and maybe prices for your latest artworks. A difficult decision for most artists is how much to show:
   1. Your recent unsold artworks.
   2. Your older unsold artworks.
   3. Artworks that have been sold, donated, or given to others.
   4. Artwork in different styles, series, or mediums.

At a minimum you should show full (800-pixel-wide on a big screen) images of your latest unsold artwork, one artwork to a page. Below each image should be a three-paragraph description of what inspired you to create the artwork; how it was produced; and details of size, materials, etc.

The description section, as with everything else you write, must be interesting and presented in a storytelling style. Keep empathy with prospective collectors by relating your inspiration as though you were talking with them face-to-face.

I always include the full retail price. Some artists may be restricted by agreements they have with their galleries. (Pricing considerations are discussed in an earlier chapter.)

You must include a method of moving from page to page through your portfolio. I use two methods: a predetermined path with forward and backward buttons on each artwork page, taking the visitor from one artwork to the next; and a second method consisting of a matrix of buttons, showing small thumbnail images of all my artworks, where the visitor may select which artwork page to jump to next.

In addition, I have a separate page with an index of my artworks by title. Each title links to the page in my portfolio that displays and describes that particular artwork. I have frequently found that prospective collectors look for artworks by title as well as by appearance.

Your "Contact Me" page:

This is all about how a prospect may reach you. You should include your email address and a phone number.

Putting this data directly into a web page can be dangerous. The website may be scanned by spammers to extract this information for use in sending you unsolicited messages. There is an easy way to minimize this issue: publish the data as JPG images. Separately write the phone number and the email address in a suitable word processing application, and save the writings as JPG images. Post these images into your web page.

I use the phone number of my mobile phone so that I can answer inquiries directly. Remember, you always want to minimize friction.

Your "About Me" pages:

This is all about you. I include an image of me at work, an artist's statement, and a detailed biography.

Also, I include links to testimonials by my collectors, and a link to a frequently updated web page that lists where my artwork may be currently viewed, including an invitation to make an appointment to visit my studio. I also include links to press releases and videos about me, my art activities, and my artwork.

Your "How to Buy My Artwork" page:

Your prospect is ready to buy. Make sure that it is easy. I ask the prospective buyer to contact me directly by phone or email. There we may discuss taxes, packing, shipping, and method of payment. (See the discussion in an earlier chapter on handling payments.)

Content, design, etc.:

To keep your prospective collector looking at your website, your messages must have great content. They must be interesting and generous with information, and always include a call for action. More on this topic may be found in an earlier chapter.

To sum up the previous discussions, your website must include:
1. One or more landing pages.
2. Your portfolios, including images, descriptions, a way to steer through the web pages, plus (most likely) prices and an artwork name index.
3. "About You" pages, including an image, an artist's statement, and a biography.
4. How to contact you, with email address, phone number, events (where to see your artwork currently on show), and an invitation to visit your studio.
5. How to sign up for your newsletter.
6. How a prospective customer can purchase one or more of your artworks.

In addition, I have a section titled "How I Do It." This consists of a number of articles I have written over the years:

Painting Techniques
    1. On developing a painting.
    2. My palette.
    3. On painting with gouache.

Painting Styles
    1. Portraits.
    2. Crowd scenes.

The Finished Painting
    1. The back of the painting.
    2. Scanning my painting.

Commissions
    1. Memorializing paintings.
    2. Portraits.

Of these, "On Painting with Gouache" is a bestseller, attracting twenty-five or more visitors from all over the world each day.

The landing page and subsequent pages of each article require careful design, if you wish to encourage visitors to explore other pages of your website. A recent study showed that 74 percent of online readers get frustrated with websites if the content they see has nothing to do with their interests. [48] So be careful not to promise in your titles more than you are able to deliver. [49]

Keywords:

Keywords are used by search engines such as Google, Bing, and Yahoo to determine the subject matter of your web page. But you may help your web page be found in a search by using commonly used words to describe your artwork in your web content. Think how you would ask about your artwork if you were searching.

The search engines are very clever and know if you're trying to game the system by overusing certain words. So be careful.

Building your website:

The easiest but most expensive path is to find an outside (preferably local) service to build your website. If you follow this path, ensure that the designer is familiar with responsive design and the concept of friction from links.

Another path is to use any of several full-service websites. [50] [51] With these, the setup is very straightforward, and they provide guidelines, instructions, and hosting. You pay by the month, with several levels of service. For the lower-priced services you do not have a simple domain name but are listed as http://www.yourname.servicename.com. At a higher level, and for an additional fee, you usually have your own domain name.

On a more do-it-yourself path, several service websites provide online website builders—some paid [52] and some free [53].

I took an even more do-it-yourself approach. I purchased Adobe's Dreamweaver [54] application and taught myself with the help of online training videos [55]. This is a long, time-consuming, and expensive path. But I have been using computers for many years.

Test before you jump:

No matter which path you take, test the offered sample website landing pages on your computer screen, on your tablet, and on your smartphone.

Are they quick to load and easy to read without scrolling sideways, resizing the images and type size for each screen size (that is, they use responsive design)?

Is the attention-grabbing content at the top? How many friction-generating clicks are there to reach the images in the portfolio?

Watch out for designs that are flashy but may not be useful or attractive to your prospective collectors. Also, remember that Flash video cannot be viewed on an iPad or iPhone.

Some other items to keep in mind:

1. Be sure that your finished website uses the principles of responsive design (other proprietary descriptive names may be used).
2. Use a shallow design to reduce friction. That is, use as few clicks (links)one or two maximum–as possible from your landing page to reach your message, such as your portfolio images.
3. When using images, make use of the "alt tag." Many smartphone users turn off the display of images to save the cost of data downloads when looking at emails and browsing the web. The alt tags are a method of having words instead of your image displayed on the smartphone or tablet screen. Learn how to insert these tags for all of your web images. Your message will have more meaning if these words appear when the images are suppressed. Also, search engines may read these tags.
4. Learn about "meta tags." These are pieces of invisible information that appear in the code at the top of each web page. There are quite a few, but the ones you should know about are "description tags" and "keywords tags."

Your website designer or service will assist you in learning
how to enter and use these tags.

Measuring performance:

You have your website up and working. You hope that people are viewing
your hard work. A variety of tools exist to help you along the way. Very
often your hosting service will provide some free tools. In addition, there
are some free stand-alone services. [56] [57]

At their simplest level, these services count for you the number of "hits" on
your website and often on each web page. This refers to the number of people
who, even for a fraction of a second, looked at your web page. If a person
goes away and returns to a web page, each visit counts as a separate hit.

A more useful measure is "unique visitors." This records how many different
people over a time period came to visit a specific web page or website.

Another useful report is "visitor path." This records each web page that
the visitor looked at when visiting your website. Often this is coupled
with how long the visitor stayed at each page.

A different free report [58] provides data on how long your website was not
available—the downtime (or the inverse—the uptime) of your website host.

Advertising on your website:

Another income path is to add a block of advertising to your web page.
A simple and free approach is to use Google Adwords. [59] Of course, this
adds some spam to your web pages, but it is discreet and up to you.

Summary:

1. Carefully choose your hosting service and domain name.
2. Many of your prospective collectors use smartphones and tablets. Understand the principals of responsive design.
3. Carefully design your landing page and your artwork portfolio.
4. Make it easy to contact you, to learn about you, and to know how to buy from you.
5. Choose a path to build your website. Test carefully the given sample web pages before you commit.
6. Continually measure your website's performance.

Here is where to start: If you do not feel capable of building your own website, get outside help, either locally or online. Always test the offered sample websites. You are becoming an expert now.

EPILOGUE

After reading this book, hopefully you will realize the challenges to be overcome in successfully marketing yourself and your artworks as a professional visual artist.

All of this is taking place in a continually changing environment that requires watchfulness and feeding. To help you, I have created a blog about this book (http://peterworsleymarketingbook.wordpress.com) where you may comment about the book's content, obtain links to new material, updates to the links in the notes, read my afterthoughts, and perhaps give me a formal review.

For the few who venture forth, the rewards will more than justify the hard work needed.

Good wishes.

PETER WORSLEY

NOTES

Introduction

1. Jason Horejs, "Taking the Leap: Making Art Your Full-Time Profession," *Reddotblog*, September 11, 2013, http://www.reddotblog. com/wordpress/index.php/taking-the-leap-making-art-your-full-time-profession.

Chapter 1: Branding

2. McCarthy, Ondaatje, Brooks, and Szanto, *A Portrait of the Visual Arts: Meeting the Challenges of a New Era, Monogram 290*: Rand Corporation, 2005). http://www.rand.org/pubs/monographs/MG290. html.

3. Gregory Peters, "Branding 101 for Artists," *Empty Easel*, March 2, 2009, http://makingamark.blogspot.com/2009/03/8th-march-2009-whos-made-mark-this-week.html.

Chapter 2: Outbound Marketing

4. Seth Godin, "Interruption Marketing," *Seth Godin*, August 10, 2013, http://sethgodin.typepad.com/seths_blog/2008/01/permission-mark. html.

5. *Chuck Green's Design Briefing*, Issue 165. www.ideabook.com.

6. Jason Horejs, "Does It Make Sense to Show Your Art in Commercial (Consignment) Galleries?," *Reddotblog*, October 8, 2013, http:// www.reddotblog.com/wordpress/index.php/make-sense-show-art-commercial-consignment-galleries.

7. Jason Horejs, "Is Showing Your Art in a Co-op Gallery Worthwhile?," *Reddotblog*, October 2, 2013, http://www.reddotblog.com/wordpress/index.php/worthwhile-showing-art-co-op-gallery.

8. Jason Horejs, "Should Artists Show Their Art in 'Vanity' Galleries?," *Reddotblog*, September 25, 2013, http://www.reddotblog.com/wordpress/index.php/artists-show-art-vanity-gallery.

9. Quote from Rebecca Wilson, director Saatchi Gallery. Alex Hudson, "June 2013. *Art 'sold more online than in galleries,'*". reported by Alex Hudson, June 26, 2013. BBC Click, June 26, 2013,. (http://www.bbc.co.uk/news/technology-23054641).

10. *"Amazon Makes Splash in Online Art Sales,." Fine Art Today/Fine Art Connoisseur*, August 18, 2013, (http://www.fineartconnoisseur.com/Amazon-Makes-Splash-in-the-Online-Art-Sales-Space/17063231).

11. *"EmailEmail Is Crushing Twitter, Facebook for Selling Stuff Online,"* *Wired, July 2013,*. (www.wired.com/business/2013/07/emailemail-crushing-twitter-facebook/.)

12. "QR Codes," *Wikipedia.com,* http://en.wikipedia.org/wiki/QR_code.

13. *Bloomberg Business Week*, October 18, 2013: 96.

14. Corey Eridon, "How to Choose a Solid Topic for Your Next Blog Post," *Hubspot*, October 19, 2013, http://blog.hubspot.com/marketing/how-to-choose-solid-topic-next-blog-post-ht.

15. Corey Eridon, "What the Best Business Bloggers Do (And You Should Too)," *Hubspot*, September 25, 2013, http://blog.hubspot.com/marketing/blogging-best-practices-list.

16. Tehmina Zaman. "Blogger vs. WordPress," *Epreneur TV* 12 May 2013. http://www.epreneur.tv/blogger-v-wordpress-the-best-blog-platform.

17. Jay Acunzo and Anum Hussain, "An Introduction To Google+ For Business," *HubSpot*, http://www.scribd.com/mobile/doc/151849412.

18. "How to Sell Your Art on Pinterest," www.pinterest.com/artistsinfo.

19. Ginny Soskey, "Pinterest Lead Generation 101," October 10, 2013, *HubSpot*, http://blog.hubspot.com/marketing/how-to-generate-leads-with-pinterest-ht.

20. "A Guide to Pinterest's New Buiness Accounts," *HubSpot*, http://offers.hubspot.com/guide-to-pinterests-new-business-accounts.

21. "PINTEREST HAS 70 MILLION USERS MORE THAN 70% ARE IN THE U.S." *Semiocast*, July 10, 2013. http://semiocast.com/en/publications/2013_07_10_Pinterest_has_70_million_users.

22. *Richrelevance*, April 26, 2013, http://www.richrelevance.com/blog/2013/04.

23. Allen Gannett, "Marketing Where They Don't Belong? 5 B2B Brands Driving Results With Instagram," *Hubspot*, October 3, 2013, http://blog.hubspot.com/marketing/b2b-brands-driving-results-instagram-ht.

Chapter 3: Inbound Marketing

24. Susannah Fox. *Pew Internet: Health*. Pew Research Center, http://www.pewinternet.org/Commentary/2011/November/Pew-Internet-Health

25. "You Can't Sell Your Art Until You Learn How to Sell It." *Art Business*. http://www.artbusiness.com/consultpurp.html.

26. Marisa Smith, "How to Develop a Strong Inbound Company Culture." *The Whole Brain Group*, September 19, 2013, http://blog.hubspot.com/marketing/develop-inbound-culture-var.

27. Chad Pollitt, "A Marketer's Guide to Getting Started With Personalization," *DigitalRelevance* (blog), September 12, 2013, http://blog.hubspot.com/marketing/marketers-guide-get-started-content-personalization.

Chapter 4: Writing Content

28. Pamela Vaughan, "10 Ways to Make Your Content More Fun to Read," *HubSpot*, October 2, 2013. http://blog.hubspot.com/marketing/how-to-make-content-fun-to-read-list.

29. David Lavenda, "Time at the Office: 10 Story Telling Tips to Help You Be More Persuasive," *FastCompany*. http://www.fastcompany.com/3015140/leadership-now/once-upon-a-time-at-the-office-10-storytelling-tips-to-help-you-be-more-persu.

30. Robert McKee, "*Storytelling That Works*," *Harvard Business Review.*, http://hbr.org/2003/06/storytelling-that-moves-people.

31. "Powerful Value Propositions," *Marketing Experiments*, September 18, 2013, www.marketingexperiments.com.

32. Ginny Soskey, "Is Social Media Killing Brands?," *HubSpot*, September 12, 2013, http://blog.hubspot.com/marketing/is-social-media-killing-brands-tl.

Chapter 5: Closing the Sale

33. Jason Horejs, "How Do You Ask for the Close When Selling Art," *RedDotBlog*, August 29, 2013, http://www.reddotblog.com/wordpress/index.php/how-do-you-ask-for-the-close-when-selling-art-collective-wisdom.

34. Closing Sales. *Wikipedia.* http://en.wikipedia.org/wiki/Closing_(sales).

Chapter 6: Your Computer, Software, and Accessories

35. Continuous Flow Ink Systems. *Wikipedia.* http://en.wikipedia.org/wiki/Continuous_ink_system.

36. Peter Worsley, "On Scanning My Paintings: An Alternative to Digitally Photographing Your Paintings," *Peter Worsley Website*, http://www.peterworsley.com/About_Me/On_Scanning_My_Paintings.html.

Chapter 7: Working with Images

37. Gary W. Priester. "Consistent Colors For Your Site - All You Need To Know About Web Safe Colors." *HTMLGoodies.* http://www.htmlgoodies.com/tutorials/web_graphics/consistent-colors-for-your-site-all-you-need-to-know-about-web-safe-colors.html.

38. "Your First Step to Accurate Color." Xrite Photo Screen Color Calibration. http://www.xritephoto.com/ph_learning.aspx?action=display&gclid=CN3p6O7Vv7oCFc1xQgodG00AOQ.

Chapter 8: Using Email

39. Sara Davidson, "Emails Not Getting Into Your Lists' Inboxes?," *HubSpot*, October 2, 2013, http://blog.hubspot.com/marketing/emails-try-focusing-on-engagement-ht.

40. Ginny Soskey, "The Go-to Guide to Creating Email Newsletters People Actually Read," *HubSpot*, August 20, 2013, http://blog.hubspot.com/marketing/guide-creating-email-newsletters-ht.

41. Dan Zarrella "The Science of Email Marketing 2012." *Hubspot.* http://www.slideshare.net/HubSpot/the-science-of-email-marketng.

42. Pamela Vaughan, "33 Examples of Dynamic Tags to Personalize Your Email Sends," *HubSpot*, Junee 22, 2012, http://blog.hubspot.com/blog/tabid/6307/bid/33315/33-Examples-of-Dynamic-Tags-to-Personalize-Your-Email-Sends.aspx.

43. "Secret Formula for Subject Lines." *MailChimp.* October 29, 2013. http://kb.mailchimp.com/article/how-do-i-know-if-im-writing-a-good-subject-line/

Chapter 9: Your Website

44. "How to Choose a web Host." *WikiHow.* http://www.wikihow.com/Choose-a-Web-Host

45. Christopher Heng. "Tips on Choosing a Good Domain Name." *The site wizard.* http://www.thesitewizard.com/archive/domainname.shtml

46. "Adobe Digital Marketing Insights," January 20, 2012, (http://bgr.com/2012/01/20/tablet-owners-spend-50-more-per-purchase-online-than-smartphone-owners/)

47. John Paul Mains, "Marketing Land: How to Design a Landing Page That Converts," *Marketing Land*, http://marketingland.com/how-to-design-a-landing-page-that-converts-57236.

48. "Online Consumers Fed Up with Irrelevant Content on Favorite Websites, According to Janrain Study" *Janrain*. 31 July 2013. http://janrain.com/about/newsroom/press-releases/online-consumers-fed-up-with-irrelevant-content-on-favorite-websites-according-to-janrain-study/

49. Meghan Keaney Anderson, "How to Use Dynamic Content for 'Smarter' Marketing, *Hubspot*, September 6, 2013., http://blog.hubspot.com/marketing/how-to-use-dynamic-smart-content-im-ht.

50. FolioSnap. (www.foliosnap.com)

51. ARTsala. (www.artsala.com)

52. Ultimate website Builder. (www.ultimatwb.com)

53. BlueVoda website Builder. (www.bluevoda.com)

54. Dreamweaver. {www.adobe.com/mena_en/products/dreamweaver.html}

55. Lynda. (www.lynda.com)

56. StatCounter. (www.statcounter.com)

57. Google Analytics. (wwww.google.com/analytics)

58. InternetSeer LLC. (www.internetseer.com)

59. Google AdWords. (www.google.com/adwords}

Epilogue

INDEX

ABOUT THE AUTHOR

Born and educated near London, England. In the 1950s, Peter Worsley moved to the United States when he took a job in Santa Monica, California. For many years he worked in marketing and communications with high-tech people, products, and ideas. Peter retired in 1996 while living in Santa Barbara. Seeking a change of pace, he set out on a path to become a professional artist painter.

Today, in his mideighties, he sees himself as a kind of old soul and romantic at heart. The subjects he chooses to paint have some sort of nostalgic calling—ordinary people doing everyday things at interesting places. Often the result is a moving painting reflecting the human comedy.

Recently, as he spoke with other artists, it became clear that many do not realize what it takes to market their artworks. With the rapidly changing environment of the Internet and other related means of communication, the so-called "tried-and-true" methods of yesteryear are no longer adequate.

With this insight, Peter decided to give back to the art community, first by hosting several workshops, and then by writing this book.

www.ingramcontent.com/pod-product-compliance
Lightning Source LLC
Chambersburg PA
CBHW051331170526
45166CB00002B/775